DIFFERENTIATION SELLING®

A Practical Guide to Selling Services and Solutions in Competitive Markets

By René Knecht

Differentiation Selling®

ISBN: 978-90-8159-944-3 (Printed Version)

Differentiation Selling®
A Practical Guide to Selling Services and Solutions in Competitive Markets

First Edition, printed version in English.

Published by René Knecht
Differentiation Selling®
Jozef Plateaustraat 11
B-9000 Gent
Belgium
www.differentiationselling.com
mail: info@differentiationselling.com

ISBN   **ISBN: 978-90-8159-944-3 (Printed Version)**
NUR   802
Wettelijk Depotnummer: D/2012/Rene Knecht, uitgever
Legal Depot : D/2012/Rene Knecht, publisher

Differentiation Selling®

Differentiation Selling is Registered in US Patent and Trademark Office.
Differentiation Selling is Registered in The Benelux Office for Intellectual Property (BOIP)

Preface

This book aims to provide you with a useful method (*Differentiation Selling*) that you can apply to your own sales context. The various stages are not always presented in a logical order, but are described as a procedure. We have not tried to write a work of literature, but rather to explain this method as best as possible from various angles. This means you can just read the chapters that are relevant for you.

It covers so-called *tacit knowledge*: knowledge gained in practice that cannot be explained in models or concepts. We call it a sales learning method, which we know from experience is effective.

The concept of the three time dimensions and process-oriented questions were developed in the first book (Dutch edition, 2010, Kluwer, 2011), and this concept is also used in this tutorial.

The emphasis is on the question of how to sell using the *Differentiation Selling* method. We refer to the literature study at the end for explanations and correlations with *best practices* in, for example, change management, conflict management and leadership.

We received valuable feedback from participants in the *Differentiation Selling seminars,* and so have been able to reformulate the concept of *Differentiation Selling* as a learning method in an *on-going* process that strives for continuous improvement.

Examples of using process-oriented questions

> **Appendix 1** contains a list of the most frequently asked process-oriented questions.
> **Appendix 2** contains an example of a sales conversation with process-oriented questions in the IT personnel-outsourcing sector.
> **Appendix 3** contains an example of a sales conversation with process-oriented questions for selling a financial solution.
> **Appendix 4** contains further examples of process-oriented questions for *entrepreneurial selling*.

> **Appendix 5** contains another approach to the concept of *selling value*.

How do you read this book?

We have deliberately kept this book concise. If you prefer to learn from practical experience and then understand the background later, you can start by reading the examples in appendices 1, 2 and 3, and then read the book from chapter I.

Glossary

Process Power

> The influence gained from the selling method used or the way in which the *sales process* is managed. Verbal (asking questions) and non-verbal tactics are used. For example, asking process-oriented questions provides *process* power: you lead the conversation and the interaction. You enable the client to come to their own conclusions that their current method or supplier is no longer adequate, which in turn leads to the client making their own commitment. The client is influenced by the seller, moves towards the seller's way of thinking, and starts to become the requesting party.

> *Tip*: An indication that you are losing the *process power* is when the client starts to control the conversation (Who is leading the conversation and determining the next step? Who is asking questions? Who is giving everything away?)

Cooperative Process or Creating Interaction

> The management of all variables so that the client can enter into a dialogue with the seller. The seller ensures they have the client's full attention. They do this by ensuring they start by asking (process-oriented) questions and listening to the client's answers, and then allowing the client to also ask questions, and listening to them. *See also Process Power and Dialogue.*

Expert Power

The influence one obtains through knowledge and experience or through arguments. Juniors normally have very little *expert power* and could compensate with *process power*. Answers to process-oriented questions gives Expert Power: the client will tell the seller all the reasons why he would like to change.

Dialogue

Two-way communication using the *give* (listen) *and receive* principle, i.e. there is a balance.

In a dialogue, the client will also ask questions and listen. The dialogue is created when there is mutual respect and trust. The client must therefore also have the freedom to say 'yes' or 'no'. If the seller directs the client towards a 'yes' answer, there is manipulation and the dialogue ends. If there is a lack of balance between giving and receiving, there will be no sale. Only asking questions is not sufficient; the client must also ask questions and listen. There must be both verbal and non-verbal interaction and momentum. The seller must create a cooperative process. *Refer to Process Power and Cooperative Process.*

Hunting or Cold Acquisition

The selling process for recruiting new clients or selling new products/services to an organization. For this to be successful, you will need to overcome certain patterns (in buying, criteria, opinions, buying behaviour etc.). Process-oriented questions are a *tool* for this.

Process-oriented questions

Questions that investigate the client's motives, how that person makes decisions, either in the past, present or future. These questions are useful for creating a dialogue, and provide an opportunity to break certain patterns. Process-oriented questions focus on the HOW; they give the decision-making process a boost. The most important characteristic of process-oriented questions is forcing the client to think about his/her decisions and motives. The change can be created in this moment of standstill.

Disturbing questions or provocative questions

A technique for using questions to create a sense of slight unease or cognitive dissonance. This can lead to clients accepting your vision, product or service, although they may also reject it.

We use provocative questions to query assumptions or presumptions that maintain the status quo. These provocative questions are only effective if you have first created uncertainty about past decisions using process-oriented questions. If this is not the case, you will receive answers that are too vague, because the client won't have fully considered the status quo.

Cognitive dissonance

Cognitive dissonance is a discomfort caused by holding conflicting cognitions (e.g. ideas, beliefs, values, emotional reactions) simultaneously. In a state of dissonance, people may feel surprise, dread, guilt, anger, or embarrassment. The theory of cognitive dissonance in social psychology proposes that people have a motivational drive to reduce dissonance by altering existing cognitions, adding new ones to create a consistent belief system, or alternatively by reducing the importance of any one of the dissonant elements. (source: *Wikipedia*)

Without this dissonance phase, the client's attitude will not change. The dissonance creates a creative tension. However, research into communication has shown that this dissonance should not be too great.

Commodity

Services or products where the client experiences no difference between the various suppliers. In this case, price can play an important role in the buying decision. It concerns the client's perception, not the seller's. Good quality *consultancy* companies might also be perceived as *commodity*. An indication for a commodity market is that a client already knows what they need before a sales discussion takes place. The decision-making criteria are pre-determined.

Solution Sales

This concerns services or products whose value is not yet obvious to the client. The concept still needs to be created. The seller creates a cooperative process for this, for example by asking targeted questions. Asking specific questions creates value (forms the solution) during the sales discussion.

Top Advisor

This type of seller advises the client, who may or may not accept the advice. They are usually seller-advisors, experts or specialists that create added value for the client because of their knowledge and experience. Process-oriented sales skills are also important for Top Advisors, because 'being right' is not the same as 'being proved right'. Creating a dialogue puts you in a better position to provide the client with your solution or advice.

Entrepreneurial Selling

Type of sale where the seller collaborates with the client to consider their (the client's) clients. Process-oriented questions can also be an excellent tool for creating value in the sales process.

Value

Value = Revenues – Costs. A sale is created when a concept or personal experience creates value for the client. Every deal has its costs alongside its objective and subjective revenues and benefits. Objective costs are, for example, costs from investments or other expenses related to change. Subjective costs include the discomfort or stress caused by change as perceived by the client. If the client considers these costs to be too high, it can result in a deal not going through.

Contents

I. Differentiation Selling: Why? What? How?

Why Differentiation Selling?

The client is looking for a supplier, not a solution.

Have you ever experienced a situation when you could have solved a client's problem, but they didn't seem open to your proposal or even want to listen? This happens to many service providers, and is caused by the tendency towards commoditization in sectors such as Finance, HR, IT, consultancy, and professional service provision since the start of the 21st century. The client sees very little difference between the various suppliers, so the **decision-making criteria** for selecting a supplier is more or less decided in advance: the prospect already knows what he wants. This can make it very difficult for suppliers to start a dialogue about possible **problem areas** that you could solve, because the client has already considered this and made a decision about what they need.

Every company has a number of unique benefits or strong points that could provide added value for the client, but the client has not been convinced about this and does not see any difference between the various suppliers.

Convincing the client about your added value: easy?

A solution's added value can simply be the difference between its Revenues and Costs. But how do you convince the client about this?

Added value = Revenues – Costs

Revenues

Examples of objective revenues are:

▸ **ROI, profit, savings, market share ...**
The highlighting of 'positive' returns usually has very little impact on the client, and so is not particularly efficient. They are definitely important requirements, but not a trigger for action or change.

▸ **Avoiding loss or risk (*Selling the pain*)**
Emphasizing the prevention of problems creates a certain degree of tension and can be more efficient, but is still not generally sufficient to inspire the client into action or change. Asking a smoker what consequences smoking has on their health, for example, normally has very little effect.

▸ Subjective returns
There are also the more subjective returns such as reputation, career, security, power, ego, etc. You might call these 'hidden agendas', and they can indeed promote sales, but they can also be a hindrance.

Even if we focus only on revenues, we will notice that some clients still show resistance. So let us also consider the costs.

Costs

▸ **Investment cost** is not usually deemed to be a problem, providing that the revenues exceeds the costs.
▸ **Cost of changing from one supplier to another** delays the sales process and creates internal resistance.
▸ **Risks** involved with making buying decisions are very important to so-called risk-shy 'mainstream clients'. This creates the need for references, and for reliable (or renowned) sellers who listen.
▸ **Subjective costs** , such as the stress or pain of change, overcoming internal resistance to change, and wanting it.

The more emotional and subjective costs often result in persistent resistance from the client, which cannot be penetrated by logical arguments. Something that was urgent yesterday isn't today! Changing the status quo is the seller's biggest challenge *("Do we want it hard enough?").*

The client must be given the opportunity to change their attitude

This means change must be made as comfortable as possible for the client. Brain research has shown that the cause of our desire for conformity comes from the evolution of our reptile brain. Humans smell danger in every change and so develop resistance. In his book 'The Dip', Seth Godin explains why our society always strives for mediocrity, and why innovation is avoided or punished. Most clients simply don't want something that is new, better or faster.

Selling is a *change management* process

Change is created in dialogue, in a moment of standstill. So timing is essential here. As a seller, you can easily learn the skills required for creating a cooperative process, where you offer the client the opportunity to make a decision.

This decision can be to your benefit, or to your detriment. You will need to learn to accept the latter, because otherwise there can be no room or freedom for making a decision, and so also no dialogue. And without any dialogue, there can be no sale.

The seller is the changing factor.

What is Differentiation Selling?

Changing the status quo is the seller's biggest challenge

For every client gained by the seller, there is a moment in time when that client changed their buying criteria. Buying criteria are the reasons or expectations that formed the basis upon which decisions have been made in the past to use the current working method. In 'Differentiation Selling', we call this the client's status quo: the current situation is the result of a decision taken in the past. When a seller approaches a client with a new proposal, they ask the client to revise their status quo. Sometimes this works, but resistance to change is normally too high. When approaching clients directly, you traditionally end up with *closing* percentages of 10 to 20 percent. This is by and large the percentage of successful change processes within organizations.

This brings us to the heart of the matter: selling is a change management process.

It can be illustrated as follows:

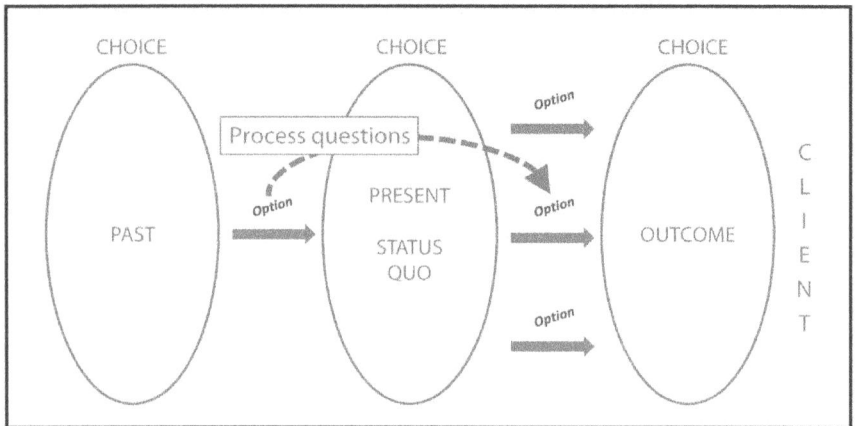

©2010 René Knecht

The client's current situation, the status quo, is the result of a decision taken in the past.

If you want to change the current situation, the client will first need to reconsider and re-evaluate a decision they have taken in the past.

How do you deal with this as seller?

Traditionally, sellers have tried to understand clients so that they can investigate the reasons for change together. Sellers often used to use 'push models', but nowadays most sellers believe it is more important to listen. This show that you are focusing on the client and trying to consider their needs. However, because there is now a clear tendency towards commoditization, this is no longer sufficient in current markets. Clients experience very little contextual (product characteristics) or procedural (sales processes) differences between various suppliers. This means the decision-making criteria used to choose a supplier are basically already determined in advance: the prospect knows what they want. They have experience with your type of service provision, and no longer listen to you, so there is no dialogue. This means the market becomes *procurement driven*. The procurement criteria are predetermined, and the client wants to make a comparison (*"Send me an offer"*).

The change is made between the ears

People are not keen on changing their opinions, and prefer instead to believe they are right. You don't persuade clients with *facts & figures*; they have to convince themselves, otherwise there is no 'commitment'. *They might say "Call me next week", but then when you try you won't be able to reach them. This is what makes selling so difficult, even if you are offering tailor-made solutions that will genuinely help the client.*

Every company of course has a number of unique benefits or strengths that differentiate them from their competitors, but the client does not necessarily recognize this; they have, after all, already formed their opinion.

Traditional sales techniques, almost all of which are based on avoiding 'pain', lose their efficiency. They are used by almost all sellers, and clients basically suffer from *solutions fatigue*. Methods such as these also meet with resistance because they prescribe change, and so are (slightly) manipulative.

> **Clients are generally not open to change (the cause of their resistance) so we first need to make the change negotiable (overcome the status quo).**

Differentiation Selling is a method that the seller learns in order accomplish the following:

1. focus 100% on the client
2. make 'change' negotiable
3. get the client to make a decision

The content (= the solution) will then follow automatically.

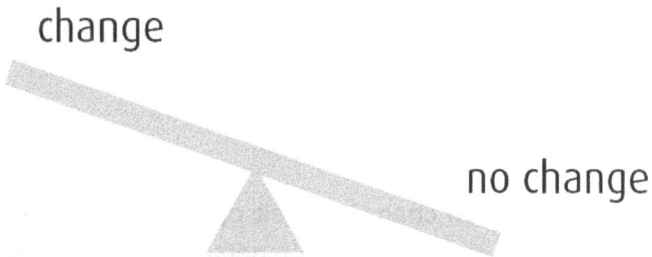

change

no change

©2010 René Knecht

The seller guides the client through the choice of 'change' or 'no change'.

*Hunting, cold acquisition or the process of recruiting new clients essentially means **breaking patterns**. The client will have to consider a new solution and/or a new supplier, and will need to make a final decision: **to change (closing) or not to change**.*

Hunting is the skill that is most sought after when recruiting sellers

Differentiation Selling is a method that first makes it possible to negotiate the STATUS QUO. This is a radical break from traditional ideas on selling.

Examples of questions it's best <u>NOT</u> to ask

- ▸ *"Do you think it's important to ..." (aimed at the future: you are already discussing the solution, before the client is ready for it)*
- ▸ *"What would the consequences be if you did not resolve this?" (aimed at the future, manipulative: you are exerting pressure, trying to sell, pushing the client into a corner)*

These questions should only be asked once the client has decided they want to change. This often happens automatically in the Differentiation Selling method, which is why we use process-oriented questions.

Questions that you <u>CAN</u> ask

- ▸ *"How did your current work method come about?" (past)*
- ▸ *"How long have you been looking ... ?" (past)*

You will experience as a seller that this gives you a different type of discussion. Because the client first has to consider their answers to these process-oriented questions, the style of communication takes on a whole new form.

How can Differentiation Selling be used?

Large organizations

We often agree contracts with large organizations, who have lots of red tape involved in their decision-making processes. Contracts and proposals for collaborations often have to pass through several different departments before they are finally approved: buying / procurement, legal, relevant business units, and then back to procurement again. This bureaucratic route is full of delaying mechanisms that can kill the deal, so we prefer to use a **sponsor** for such *large accounts*; someone who believes in our service and is convinced that change is necessary.

Business-to-business

If you are trying to sell a service to an organization in a B-to-B-environment, and you successfully convince and even possibly make your contact enthusiastic about your solution, you can still often find that you don't hear back from them. What's happened?

Your contact will have presented your proposal to their colleagues or other managers, and most probably received the following responses: *"Yes, that's probably true"*, or *"That is indeed interesting, but it's not a priority"*, or *"We're not ready for this"*. So the project is put on hold, and often dies a quiet death. After all, there are always more reasons for not changing than there are for changing. This means you don't receive any *commitment*, and you cannot *close* the deal. So it's important that your contact person can show *commitment* , in the first place by convincing themselves.

Tip: Ask questions that gets the client thinking: *"How did you get in your current situation? Why is it still being used? Why do you still work like this? Is it still successful?"*

This forces the client to think about the reasons why change is necessary. **These reasons can be your differentiators!** These are the criteria that are important for the client, and where you as seller and supplier can make a difference. We can also call this a *Unique Buying Proposition.*

The reasons for change can also be very confrontational, and have a great impact on the organization. Your contact will therefore also have to consider how to explain this to their employees, and convince them of the need for change. Your contact becomes a sponsor for your solution.

> *Differentiation Selling allows the client start by negotiating with themselves: do I want to change or do I not want to change?*

II. Process differentiation

Guide the change process with targeted questions

Compare the following contextual questions ...

- ► *"How many employees do you have?"* (content, facts & figures)
- ► *"What technology do you use for ...?"* (facts)

... with this process-oriented questions

- ► *"How did you decide to expand this service?"* (process, historical)
- ► *"Under which circumstances do you use this service/ technology?"* (How does the client decide?)
- ► *"What alternatives are you looking for?"* (create a vision)

When they answer process-oriented questions, clients form ideas or visions, challenge/examine assumptions and draw correlations. This gives them time to think, which in turn leads to decisions.

> *Process-oriented questions create interaction, which turns selling the process into a creative one.*

Compare questions that half focus (50%) on the client ...

- ► "Would you consider a solution where we ...?"

This question is manipulative, because it already includes part of the answer. The seller is steering the process. It appears that the focus is on the client, but that's only partially true. The question has a *hidden agenda*.

... with questions that fully focus (100%) on the client

- ▸ "What solutions have you already tried?"
- ▸ "How long have you been looking?"
- ▸ "How did the project start?"

Answers to questions that focus fully on the client are unpredictable! We can no longer make assumptions, and are obliged to listen.

Full focus on the client makes the dialogue extremely powerful.

How is process differentiation created?

We focus fully on the client's decision-making process.

Don't talk about yourself; otherwise you will lose the control! It will result in the client taking the lead in the conversation too soon (*"Do you do this? Can you do that? How much does it cost?"*), and sticking to their original opinion, i.e. 'no change'.

We look back on the past and ask what is preventing the change

This is the biggest **turning point** for many sellers: as a seller, we often focus too much on reasons why the client could or should change, even though they might not really want to.

Differentiation Selling guides the change process in the client's mind with carefully considered (process-oriented) questions: "What is the reason that you are still looking for...?", "Can't your current supplier solve this for you?", "What has kept you from solving the problem/implementing this solution?"

Differentiation via the sales process

Content follows process

Services and solutions are often quite similar, and clients experience very little difference between suppliers. So the real value lies in differentiation: the difference that is important to the client (or that will become important). Only the client can decide what they find really important. When this value has been expressed, the 'solution' automatically follows. Content follows process! USPs (*Unique Selling Points*) on their own are worthless, and will only help if the client definitely wants to change. You no longer need to create the solution or steer the client in the right direction. This is done together with the client; otherwise you won't have any influence. This is why interaction (dialogue) is so important.

How does it work? Life consists of making choices

- Clients (and people in general) are constantly making choices.
- Every choice involves an alternative being rejected: this causes friction/tension because you're never certain you're making the right decision. You have to negotiate with yourself. (*"Do I really want this?"*).

  In this context, we also talk about the cognitive dissonance caused by making a decision. You could see the sales process as a series of sub-decisions, which always create doubt and tension before and after making a decision. *("Did I make the right decision?")*

  http://en.wikipedia.org/wiki/Cognitive_dissonance

- The choices or eliminations (= rejection of an alternative) create tension, because there is no ideal solution!

  This is just like the concept of there being no such thing as an ideal partner or spouse. You have to make small concessions. You accept or reconsider your relationship. You might ultimately decide to leave (looking for an alternative)?

▸ The elimination (reduction of tension when you finally reach a decision) brings the decision-making criteria that are important to the client to the fore.

The client might want to amend their criteria to choose a new (your) solution. *("Why did you choose your partner at the time? Do you still feel the same way?")*

The client has probably amended their decision-making criteria and/or reviewed their relationship for their purchasing decision. This is what sellers can achieve by managing **creative tension**! The *gaps* or opportunities for change that this creates determine your ***unique buying proposition***. This is the moment when you can introduce yourself, explain your expertise and differentiators, and offer the client the opportunity to make a decision: to change or not to change? You can see this sales process as a series of consecutive mini-closings.

The seller can only guide the client in this process: they are a facilitator who is not afraid of (creative) tension and conflict! A healthy dose of assertiveness is therefore essential.

Clients negotiate with themselves about decisions made in the past
One of the requirements for selling is to question decisions made in the past. But clients will not do this spontaneously. The seller must **guide** him in this process. It is of course possible that the client will decide they don't want to change, and you have to give them this freedom, otherwise you will no longer have a dialogue. And without dialogue, there will be no change.

▸ You create tension and the room for change by confronting the client's past expectations with today's reality. The seller can guide that process. The magic of dialogue will do the rest.
▸ A seller therefore needs to start by asking questions that will get the client thinking. The client needs to negotiate with himself or herself.
▸ The value of your solution becomes apparent when it is compared with the alternatives: your *unique buying proposition* comes to the fore.

How is change created?

What causes the client to change?

▸ **Shock**

The client didn't realize the situation was so serious. *Selling the pain* can be an efficient method, but not in commoditized or competitive markets. In these markets, *pain* questions will be met with resistance. And this is logical, because the client doesn't really want to change!

▸ **Good timing**

Waiting for external events or trends that will force the client to change. This can also work, but sometimes a seller will need to wait a long time. For example, more and more companies are realizing that social media can impact their recruitment and *employer branding*, but social media has been actively used in recruitment since 2004, and its *innovator stage* has long since passed. Another disadvantage is that it's up to the client to decide what they need, which makes it more difficult for you to influence the decision-making process. You are too late.

▸ **Direct influence**

You can also try to convince the client using arguments and USPs. This can work if your business and/or solution really is better, faster and cheaper than the competition, and if the client believes you! Direct influence is rarely successful in competitive markets. The client won't use your arguments as a reason to change.

▸ **Indirect influence**

You offer the client an opportunity to decide whether change is necessary or not. You help them make a decision. You allow the client to make their own decisions. This 'indirect influence' is exactly what we mean by Differentiation Selling.

Indirect influence

Sometimes sellers know that a prospect will become a client and sign a contract after just an initial exploratory conversation. But how can they know?

- ▸ The client also asks questions. This means they are considering their status quo.
- ▸ Information is exchanged and emotions are show. The client gives verbal or non-verbal indications that they are interested.
- ▸ There is *commitment*. The client makes a promise and sticks to it. They called back or made a decision within an agreed timeframe. It is socially acceptable for a client to lie to a seller. *Commitment* tactics are therefore a very useful sales skill.

Change is created through interaction (dialogue) with the client

This question focuses on **content,** and so does the answer:

- ▷ Question: *"What type of shirt are you wearing?"*
- ▷ Answer: *"I'm wearing a silk shirt."*

This next question focuses on **process**, so the person asked has to consider their answer:

- ▷ Question: *"How did you choose this shirt?"*
- ▷ Answer: *"I opted for soft cotton, because I have sensitive skin."*

It is this consideration that provides the opportunity for change. Eventually they will compare the current situation (i.e. wearing the soft cotton) with their expectations (i.e. Is the cotton soft enough for my sensitive skin? Am I satisfied? Does it meet my expectations?) , and there's a very good chance their expectations won't have been fully satisfied, so here lies the sales opportunity.

> *One of the characteristics of questions that focus on the process is that they have unpredictable answers. But there will definitely be a dialogue, an interaction. And the interaction can create the change.*

Characteristics of a process-oriented question

A process-oriented question ...

- ▸ challenges decisions that have been made in the past, the current status quo, and plans for the future.
- ▸ focuses 100% on the client.
- ▸ creates an interaction, which is spontaneous (*"We had a good meeting."*)
- ▸ allow clients to negotiate with themselves. ("What should I choose...?" "Do I still want this?")
- ▸ has an unpredictable answer – every client will give a unique answer.

Change is a constant. Answering questions that focus on the process makes the client aware that their procurement criteria have changed. The seller is involved in the decision-making process and can contribute their content / expertise (*unique buying propositions*). Timing is very important here. The client warms to your solution and sees you as a differentiating supplier.

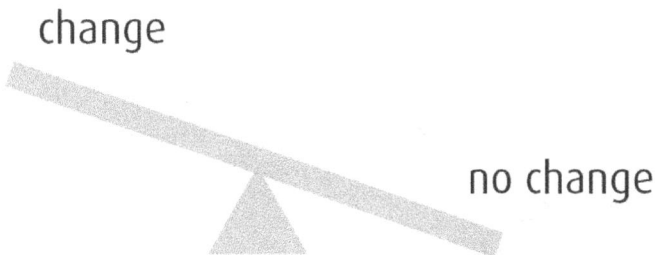

change

no change

©2010 René Knecht

With Differentiation Selling, we guide the client from not changing to changing. Timing is very important. So the sales discussion always needs to start with questions that focus on the process, and on decisions that have been made in the past. (Appendix 1 gives a summary of possible process-oriented questions in the three time dimensions).

Without dialogue, your client will form their own opinion.

Think about clients you have recruited in the past. What was the atmosphere of the discussion? What questions did the client ask? How frequently did you have contact with the client? How did the discussion evolve? How were concessions asked for and given?

Characteristics of dialogue

- Client and seller make time for each other, without time pressures or restrictions.
- Client and seller ask almost the same number of questions, in both directions.
- Client and seller listen to each other. What are the signals, verbal and non-verbal?
- There is room for to say 'yes' or 'no'. Client consciously or subconsciously defends their freedom of choice.
- The communication is regular and frequent. E-mails are answered within an acceptable timeframe. You stay in touch.
- There is a balance between giving and receiving. There is cooperation.

Characteristics of non-dialogue

- Deadlines, not enough time, interruptions
- Assurances are not met, small promises are broken
- PowerPoint presentations: how can you convince clients to change their mind if you give everything away and present cold hard facts to the client?
- Client and seller start arguing: the client wants to defend decisions they have made in the past, and stay with your competitor. Both use lot of statements.
- Without dialogue, your client will form their 'own' opinion (*"Why change: everything is fine as it is?"*) and so resist the sales process.

The client might change their opinion in the course of a dialogue. Of course, not all clients are open to change. New information that is given to clients is filtered and often rejected. The information doesn't fit in the picture. Being right is not always the same as being proven right.

> *Someone who chooses a new supplier reviews their earlier purchasing decision. This is preceded by a change process. Differentiation Selling is a method that teaches this process.*

Selling is an uncertain process, hand over the control (just like in love)

How can I convince the client?

"Are there 'tips and tricks' for convincing a client?" is a question that is always asked at seminars. It assumes the idea that the seller has to convince the client, and that they can follow a script to lead them into making the desired decision. This sounds great in theory, but in practice you are taking a chance. It might work eventually, if you try hard enough.

In uncertain situations, you look for something to hold on to

The harder a seller tries to win over a client, the easier the client will get away. You will be familiar with the situation: the client doesn't call back, or doesn't reach a decision, or – even worse – is suddenly impossible to contact. This *mindset* leads to sales organizations with a *closing ratio* of 1 in 10 or even 1 in 20. Sellers tend to be very persistent and are motivated by slogans like: *"selling starts when the client says NO"* and *"How to deal with rejection?"*

This form of scientific management based on figures feels safe. Results are predictable as long as the seller pushes hard enough. This could also explain why it's so difficult to recruit and motivate salespeople.

It doesn't work if you are selling to decision makers

Decision-makers are generally more intrinsically motivated, and have an internal reference framework. They follow their own convictions. This is also how you can recognize *decision makers*. There is no *one-size-fits-all* solution for these types of clients. Selling becomes a particularly *creative process* when you are dealing with **decision makers**, mostly at CXO level. They first want to convince themselves, so good sellers will start a cooperative process, where they allow the client to make their own decisions. If a solution is suggested too early, it will create resistance or result in you being sent back to the commodity quadrant, where you will once again be compared with the many other suppliers.

Selling as a change process is an input process, not an output process

Approximately 80 percent of output-led change processes fail: the end result does not meet expectations. Change takes place in a moment of standstill. It is an input process, not an output process. It cannot be imposed or arranged. You need (human) *commitment*, and we have no control over the human factor. Otherwise, the world would be very predictable.

This means it is better to see changes in organizations as a process of new experiences and confrontations. It is created in human interaction. Internal changes are often the result of contact with the outside world (a client, or the government or other external factors).

Selling is an uncertain process, and this is where the opportunity comes from!

When a seller focuses their questions on the client, and provides room for clients to make decisions for themselves (which they will do anyway), the answer can be unpredictable.

> ▷ Question:
> *"What have you done to solve this problem?"*

> ▷ Possible answers:
> "We are looking at what options are available in the market ..."

"We are in the final stages and will probably sign with supplier XYZ."

"We have been struggling for a year and have been in touch with three suppliers, but none of them are offering us the right solution ..."

"We are leaving our current supplier ..."

The outcome of the conversation is unpredictable and the answers can have enormous potential, as long as you listen and even forget the script... Do you have the self-confidence to do this?

So the seller manages the process rather than the script. The client's answers guide them through the decision-making process. This must happen **in consultation with the client,** at the right time, i.e. not when the client is still thinking about it, or wanting to discuss it internally. This would result in you losing your influence or *process power*, because you are handing the initiative over to the client (*"Send me a quote"*, *"Call me back next month"*) and giving them a chance to escape. It's a paradox, but to influence the process, you need to hand over the control, just like in love. This will create a *commitment* (because the client is making the decision), which in turn means you regain control. You guide the process rather than control it.

Confidence = 'guiding' rather than 'controlling'

III. Process-oriented questions and the three time dimensions

Understanding the past

There are three lines of approach when questioning the decision-making process: the past, the present and the future. In order to better understand the criteria that are important in the decision-making process, we must first concentrate on the past. We look at how clients have made decisions in the past.

- ▶ *"What was the reason for this project?" (past)*
- ▶ *"Do you have experience with ...?"*
- ▶ *"What made you decide to start this project?" (past)*
- ▶ *"Under what circumstances do you rely on ...?" (past)*
- ▶ *"How did you come to use X?" (past)*
- ▶ *"What steps have you considered for resolving this?" (past)*

Take note! It's important that you ask these questions at the beginning of the conversation (for example: see appendix 1). After all, if you start by asking future-oriented questions (*"What solution are you looking for now?"*) you immediately lose your *process power*. It will be more difficult to influence the buying criteria if you start with the 'solution image'. This does not apply if the client has already indicated they want to change, in which case you can ask a question like: *"What is the reason you are looking for a new supplier?"*

Breaking patterns

Establishing the criteria that are decisive for the client can be very effective. When the client starts to consider what is important, it becomes possible to break patterns, which is something that needs to happen to win over new clients. This means selling is a **joint learning process**, because a joint vision is created.

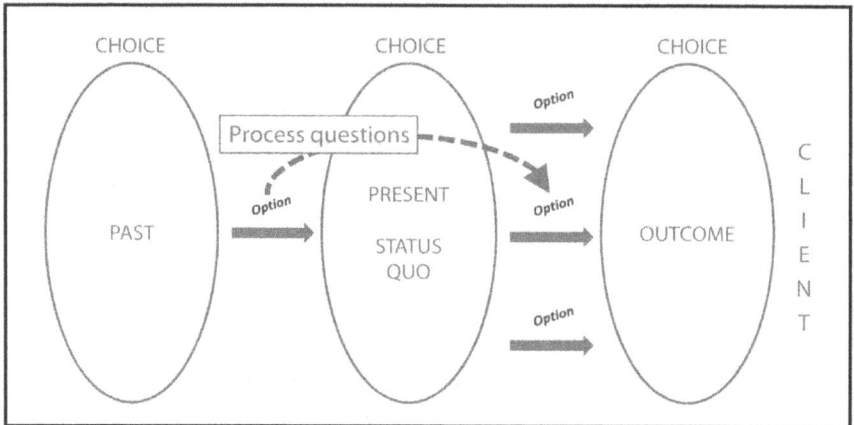

©2010 René Knecht

The client's current situation is always the result of a decision that has been taken in the past

The decision that lies at the basis of the current situation needs to be re-considered. Change is a constant. Clients' relationships, criteria and expectations change over time. This is where the opportunity lies for the seller to make the client aware of the amended criteria!

Process questions get the client thinking, so they can (possibly) revise their opinion. This can lead to further steps, for example if it seems the client is not satisfied with their current situation and requires something else: the questioning can help break patterns.

This keeps the communication process in motion. The participants in the dialogue think about past and future decisions, and this form of participative decision-making illustrates the *process power* that can generate engagement (*commitment*).

Practice

What past, present and future process questions can you ask clients in your sector?

Note and discuss with your colleagues or manager.

   Past:

   ▷ —
   ▷ —
   ▷ —

   Present:

   ▷ —
   ▷ —
   ▷ —

   Future:

   ▷ —
   ▷ —
   ▷ —

In Appendix 1 you will find a summary of past, present and future process questions that you could ask. It's important that you think about this beforehand, taking the examples we have provided into consideration. When you understand the principle, it will be easy to formulate your own questions.

Counter-examples

The technique of using counter-examples to determine the procurement criteria can be used to get a better understanding of clients' expectations and help them to decide:

- ▸ *"It seems as though everything is going fine. Are there any reasons or circumstances that would move you to consider a new supplier?"*
- ▸ *"Everything is fine … (silence)" (listen reflectively)*
- ▸ *"You already have experience with outsourcing these services. Is everything running smoothly, or is there anything you would prefer to be different?"*

You can employ the technique of using counter-example to blow life into the dialogue or get an explanation. Ask your questions in a neutral tone (not intrusive).

Tip: send an e-mail to *counterexampletechnique@differentiationselling.com* for an **audio file** with examples of such questions.

IV. Dealing with no change: you make the difference

Everlasting loyalty to a supplier is rare: is this your chance?

How did you ever decide to go and live with someone or get married ?

If you'd known then what you know now, would you have made the same decision? Are the motives that were applicable back then still applicable now? If the answer to this is NO, it doesn't mean you should get a divorce; it just means your relationship needs to change. This requires adaptation and harmonization, which can cause friction ...

The example above is one of change and conflict management in everyday life. Change is a constant. Our relationships are constantly being renewed, experienced differently, and re-assessed. It is during moments of standstill that external factors can make a breakthrough.

Moments of standstill provide sellers with a perfect opportunity

A client is often committed to a supplier and does not see any reason to change. But this commitment is the result of a decision made in the past. The motives for the original decision might have changed in the meantime. Maybe the decision-making criteria have changed a bit, or even changed drastically?

Experts and management advisors all agree that change is a constant. But yet we still generally continue to hold onto the past. We run away (*"I need to think about it"*) or resist the change (justification, counter-arguments). So it doesn't make any sense to try to *push* a client. This just hinders collaboration, so there is no longer a cooperative process. The client defends themselves. It results in long *sales cycles*, and the client ultimately never reaches a decision.

The current situation was created by a decision made in the past.

Your client's current situation, whether they are happy with or not, is the result of a decision made in the past. And the past is no longer present!

"Is everything running smoothly?
Or are there things you would like to be different?"
"What would you like to see instead?"

Clients will only take action when they really have to. They urgently need your help, but cannot reach a decision. **The art of selling lies in getting clients to discuss possible changes.**

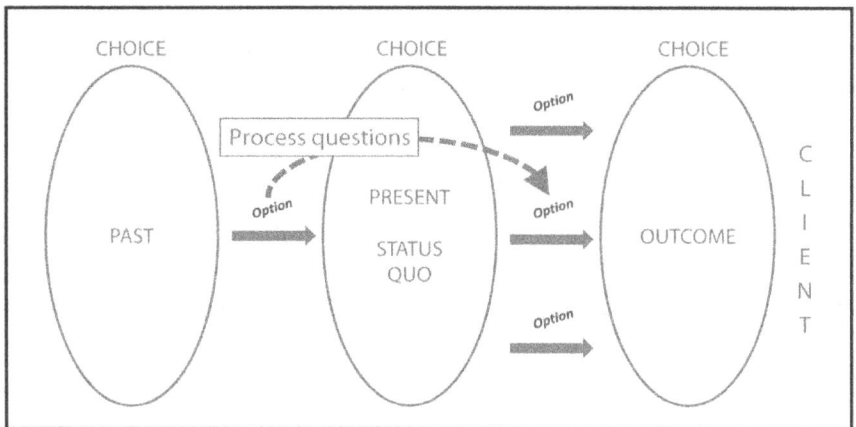

©2010 René Knecht

Help the client to review their **past** decision, which has led to the **present** situation.

Key factors

- ▸ The client's current situation is always the result of a decision that has been taken in the past.
- ▸ Change is a constant. This means the client might no longer be satisfied.
- ▸ The client will only change if the current situation no longer corresponds with the desired situation (dissatisfaction).

▸ Process-oriented questions help the client realize this. After all, clients only believe their own conclusions. The seller, as an external factor, allows the client to make a decision. (*closing=commitment*).

By focusing on what is holding the client back, we discover what the client finds really important. This is the differentiator that makes the difference to the client. We also refer to this as unique buying propositions. Comparing the alternatives during this decision-making process enables the value of your solution, in comparison to the competition or the status quo, to become clear. The client's decision-making criteria can also change in this interactive process.

V. Changing the procurement criteria

As a seller, we guide the client from a situation of not changing to one of changing. This means the client change their procurement criteria at some point during the sales process, or that the importance of certain criteria increase significantly (the problem becomes urgent), which causes them to make a procurement decision. We now go through three phases which, if the dialogue takes place between the client and the seller, follow on from each other.

PHASE 1: Aligning criteria / Go with the flow

- ▸ We first try to establish how the client's current situation came about (the past). We ask process-oriented questions in three time dimensions: the past, present and future.
- ▸ We create a cooperative environment: this means we ensure there is sufficient time and manage all environmental variables, so that we can focus fully on the client, and they have all their attention on us. Sales always take place in an interactive process.
- ▸ The dialogue will find its own momentum after a while, so it no longer needs to be 'controlled'. We could also call it 'leading' in a process of guiding and letting go.
- ▸ The 'buying criteria' can change during this process. There can be additions, with some things increasing in importance and others falling away. The client becomes aware of their dissatisfaction, because they have started to reconsider their past decisions.

change

no change

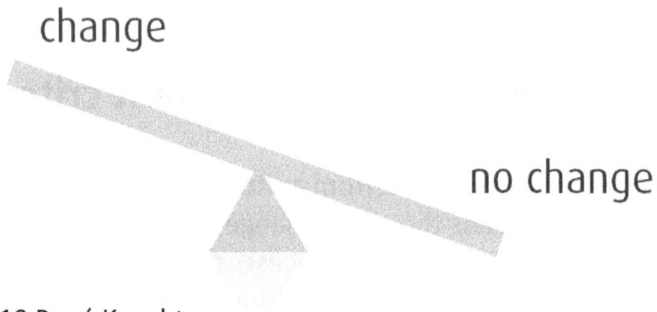

©2010 René Knecht

The seller guides the client in their decision to change or not to change. Hunting, cold acquisition, and the process of recruiting new clients are essentially the same as **breaking patterns.***The client will have to consider a new solution and/or a new supplier, and will need to make a final decision on this.* **Do we change (closing) or do we not change?**

PHASE 2: Change / Challenging criteria

- ▸ This phase starts as soon as the client starts to consider changing. The indicator is so-called 'change talk': the client starts talking about change. A vision and a picture of the future are created.
- ▸ The client asks most of the questions. There is interaction.
- ▸ The conversation evolves to consider the content of your proposal.
- ▸ The transition from phase 1 to phase 2 happens gradually and spontaneously, often almost imperceptibly.
- ▸ If the client thinks about their (former) criteria and then considers their options, the seller can propose their USPs (suggestive questions) or challenge the client's criteria (provocative questions), insofar as the client has not already done so themselves.

Suggestive questions: what if?

- ▸ *"Have you considered ...?"*
- ▸ *"Perhaps you could ...?"*
- ▸ *"What would happen if ...? (What if ...?)"*
- ▸ *"How could we use this to ...?*
  What if this method is used for ...?
  Is this also useful for sellers?"

TIMING: you respond to what the client says, not to what you are thinking. This is the only way you can 'provoke'. So don't skip over PHASE 1! In appendix 3, you will find an example of a sales conversation that illustrates this.

Provocative questions

What are the challenges in the client's sector? What questions could grab the client's attention? What are the consequences if the client stays in their status quo?

- ▸ **NOT**: *"How much can you save?"*
- ▷ **BUT**: *"How much are you currently losing every month from ...?"*
- ▸ **NOT**: *"Have you thought about a social media strategy?"*
- ▷ **BUT**: *"Are you aware that your target group is active on social media networks?"*
- ▸ **NOT**: *"Are you open to ..."*
- ▷ **BUT**: *"Considering your clientele and the changes regarding ... how are you dealing with ...?"*

Practice

Think of three *thought-provoking questions* that will grab the client's attention.

1. …
2. …
3. …

Tips:

- ▸ Think about problems that your client could incur if they don't use your solution or services.
  Example: *"How many clients have you lost because of a lack of 'sales skills'?"*

- ▸ Think about the answers you will receive to process-oriented questions that query the status quo. These are the **differentiators** (*unique buying propositions*) that are important to your client. If you, as a supplier, can answer this, you have already differentiated yourself before the competition!
  Example: *"Why hasn't it been solved?"*, *"What is the reason you are still looking?"*

- ▸ Talk the client's language and use terms such as turnover, ROI, time, budget, risk. Also think about *Entrepreneurial Selling*: process-oriented questions from the point of view of the client's client (see appendix 4). Decision-makers such as CXO are paid to have a crystal ball to guide their organization into the future. How can you help reduce the client's uncertainty?
  Example: *"What are the trends and critical business issues in your sector?"*

- ▸ *Challenge assumptions.* Ask questions that challenge assumptions / hypotheses that maintain the status quo: Why? Why not? What if?
  Examples: *"Suppose the legislation goes through. How are you going to deal with it then?"*(Assumption: the laws are set and the client might not yet have considered what consequences a change in the law could bring about, so why change?)

"Suppose there is social unrest. How will you tackle ... and keep ... safe?" (Assumption: everything remains stable, so why change?)

"How are you going to pay your mortgage if you become unable to work for 6 months?" (Assumption: I remain healthy, so why change?)

"Why is that important to you?" (The seller challenges the client's assumptions raised during the meeting)

"How will that then happen after ...?" (The seller questions whether the assumption is valid in every situation)

"Does this also apply to ...?" (Idem)

"Does your recent decision to enter this new market affect new 'sales skills'?" (Assumption: we can sell in the same way)

▸ Changing the rules: we let the client look at his presumptions from a different angle
   "Have you thought about ...?"

   *"In view of the new technology standard ...
   what happens to ...?"*

   "Are your sellers able to convince your clients to consider the change brought about by your solution?"

   "How are you going to evolve from product sales to service sales?"

▸ Challenge: what can I say or what information can I give so that the client also asks a question?
   "90% of your clientele seems to be dissatisfied with ... Do you recognize that?"

   "Clients in the ICT sector currently have different expectations from sellers ..."

   "Your target group doesn't read printed media ... only 5% of this group are still reading actual newspapers."

PHASE 3: Advance the deal

- ▸ "What is your next step?"
- ▸ What questions can you ask to make contact with other decision-makers in the buying process? Take the lead (guide): *"This is the step-by-step plan ...",*
  "Who is going to implement it? What is the impact on ...?"
- ▸ Convert vague criteria into concrete criteria. Deals are often unsuccessful because the buying criteria are not clear to everyone.
  "How will you know that something (the vision) has been achieved?
  How do you measure that? What do you mean?"
  If the client hesitates and you are unsure about your position:
  "Is there any reason why you don't want to use our solution?"
  "Why would you rather not work with an SME (Small Enterprise)?"
- ▸ *Showstoppers:* When necessary, try to eliminate any obstacles that are preventing the deal.
  "If you work like this ... it will lead to ... Is that a problem to you?"
- ▸ Ensure there is momentum and interaction: a deal in motion must stay in motion (interaction, cooperative climate).
- ▸ Sell to *large accounts*: find a sponsor.

Find a sponsor

The Differentiation Selling method is based on influencing the buying criteria. So the content comes after the process. We no longer think in terms of USPs or solutions to begin with. We first want to influence the decision-making process within the account. Large accounts can often be compared to unwieldy oil tankers: they are difficult to maneuver and lots of energy and tactics are required for it to change direction. That's why it's important with *large accounts* to know who can change the rules or direction. People with sufficient influence on decision-making can then function as a sponsor or process owner of your deal.

You also have so-called *gatekeepers* who could resist a deal: *"We're already covered", "We're already working with someone ..."* They don't have the power to change the buying criteria within the organization, but they resist change by stubbornly saying *"No"* or *"Later" (after the upgrade, after the next budget meeting, after the holidays, etc.).*

You need a sponsor who can side-step the rules, internal politics and/ or procedures. You need to identify and recruit that person.

Tips for identifying your sponsor

- ▸ The power in an organization always lies with the people who impact results (bottom line impact). Is the sponsor involved with projects that impact the organization? Sponsors don't always hold the highest positions, but they have influence because of their involvement with key projects such as product launches, restructuring, recruitment, etc.
- ▸ Is the sponsor an innovator? Are they willing to take a risk? You can also find these *risk-takers* in government and traditional mainstream companies, so it's important not to have any prejudices and not to play it safe around these clients. You are an equal sparring partner, not the favourite son-in-law.
- ▸ Do they portray the culture of the organization? Sponsors are respected and are there to protect the organization's culture. Because they have a platform (network) to work from, they can estimate what impact your solution would offer. They are often the lieutenant, the second in charge, the crown prince (or princess), the high potentials or future leaders of the company.
- ▸ Sponsors can also be external parties who have an interest in your solution (e.g. another supplier who needs your technology or services to implement his solution with the same customer) , or even your own people, e.g. project managers, who are engaged with the client and involved with the changes within their organisation.

Create commitment via your sponsor

Use your sponsor to influence other decision-makers. Deals often fall through because of people you have never spoken to. (This happens to all of us!) Minimize this risk by creating support. You can do this for example by asking good questions that create involvement and *commitment*: process-oriented questions that challenge the status quo, for example.

VI. Do not give away the process

Protect the interaction

The secret to recruiting new clients lies in interaction. How do you create a dialogue that offers the client the opportunity to revise their opinion (*"Surely everything is fine as it is?"*) or a buying decision made in the past (*"I already have a supplier"*)?

By interaction we mean every form of two-way communication, both verbal and non-verbal. Think about clients you have already recruited: how did that process go? How often did you have contact? Who contacted who? When, and how often? What questions were asked? How do you ensure you're not focusing solely on the client (ask and listen), and that the client is also focusing on you, and so also asking questions and listening? There is probably a pattern you can identify and apply to future clients.

When we talk about interaction, we think about a **flow**. Nobody is in overall control. There is a balance. The giver and receiver are equal. There is a cooperative process. This is the ideal situation and it normally develops between people who 'click', like a loved one, friends, or a good customer.

In the day-to-day sales reality, it's normally your responsibility to create this flow, which is why you need to **steer** the selling process, or even better, **guide** it, because you will also need to let go.

How can you use this in client recruitment?

Let's turn this question around. How did the client succeed in receiving concessions from us? In other words: how did the client sell themselves to us?

Perhaps...

- ▸ **they ensured several moments of contact**. They let you approach them a couple of times, and you always went home empty handed. They played with the time factor, and you cooperated.
- ▸ **they always determined the next step**, because you gave everything away. "Send me an offer", "Could you change this?", "We'll only sign if you change this", and once again, you cooperated.
- ▸ **they actively took charge of the meeting:** *"What could you do for us?", "I'll listen first …",* and you also cooperated.

In short, you gave so much of the process away that it wasn't difficult for the client to get a huge concession (content). You lost control from the beginning.

Process Power

Back to the prospecting phase. How do you ensure the client follows your steps (*process power*) and ultimately signs the order form (content, $$)?

- ▸ Listen first, before you argue (simple but true!)
- ▸ Ensure the client also asks questions.
  How can you integrate this in a demo or pre-sale phase? What can you do to integrate the interaction?

  This is what top sellers do!

- ▸ Search for a new vision together with the client (= your solution).

Creating a mutual vision ensures you get commitment. You become a business partner. This form of selling is participative decision-making. It is the result of the interaction/dialogue, as discussed previously.

VII. Most important lessons

Key factors of the Differentiation Selling method

- ▸ The client's current situation is always the result of a decision that has been made in **the past**.
- ▸ **Change** is a constant. This means it's possible the client is no longer satisfied with their way of doing things or their supplier, and the decision-making criteria are no longer up to date. The environmental factors might have changed, which can mean the client also has to change. A new environmental levy, for example, could change the buying policy for company cars. Or the motives or decision-making criteria have changed: taste changes, people want a new model, or are dissatisfied with their current supplier.
- ▸ In other words, the client will be open for change if their current situation no longer corresponds with their desired situation. This can make the client **unsatisfied** and **impatient**.
- ▸ Process-oriented questions help the **client** to see this and think about it.. After all, clients only believe their own conclusions.

How to breach the status quo?

There are two options, but we always start with the past.

The client is aware of their dissatisfaction

This will soon come up in a conversation if there is a cooperative climate / dialogue. We work with the following questions;

 ▷ **Past:**
  "How did you decide to use ... at the time?" or "Under what circumstances do you use ...?"

 ▷ **Present:**
  "What is the reason that you are looking for a new supplier / solution?"
  (maybe you could start with this, which is an advanced closing technique)

 ▷ **Future:**
  "What would you like to see instead?"

The client is not aware of their dissatisfaction

 ▷ **Past:**
  "How did you decide to use ... at the time?" or "Under what circumstances do you use ...?"

  This question forces the client to compare the past situation with the current situation. In the past, they had certain motives for choosing that solution, but because change is a constant, the situation may well have changed in the meantime.

 ▷ **Present:**
  "How's it going now?"
  (The client may or may not realize that change is necessary.)

  If the client seems reluctant, the seller can help them decide by using the counter-example technique: "Everything seems to be running smoothly ... or is there anything you would prefer to be different ... (quite monotonous, as a neutral observer, speaking calmly, without pressurizing)?"

▷ **Future:**
"What would you like to see changed?"

Change management

Only after the client has expressed their dissatisfaction (*change talk*) can the seller guide the change process, e.g. with the following questions:

▷ *"What steps have you taken to find a solution?"*
▷ *"Why hasn't it been resolved?"*
▷ *"So why are you still looking?"*
▷ *"Can your current supplier not help you with this?"*
▷ *"What do you think the next step should be?"*
▷ *"What do you need to know about us to consider us as a possible supplier?"*

These process-oriented questions provide **process power**. You are entirely focused on the client and create a dialogue. You guide the conversation from the past to the future. This means you determine the next step. The answers to the questions give **expert power**. The client states the reasons why they would change.

Typical answers are:

▷ *"We've been looking for a year, but our current partners haven't found a solution."*
▷ *"We don't have the knowledge available in house."*
▷ *"We haven't heard anything from our current supplier."*
▷ *"Our expectations haven't been met."*

This is not a script that needs to be followed exactly. Use it as a guideline to prepare for discussions. You will see that it creates magic in conversations with your clients.

Differentiation Selling®

VIII. Appendices

Appendix 1: Process-oriented questions

Past

- How long have you been looking for ...?
- Under what circumstances did you start using ...? How did you come to use...?
- How did the need for... arise?
- How did you decide...?
- What made you decide to work this way/to start this project?
- What steps have you taken or considered to resolve this problem?
- Can't your actual supplier solve this for you?
- What is the reason that you are still looking for ...? What's preventing you from solving this problem?
- Under what circumstances do you use ...?

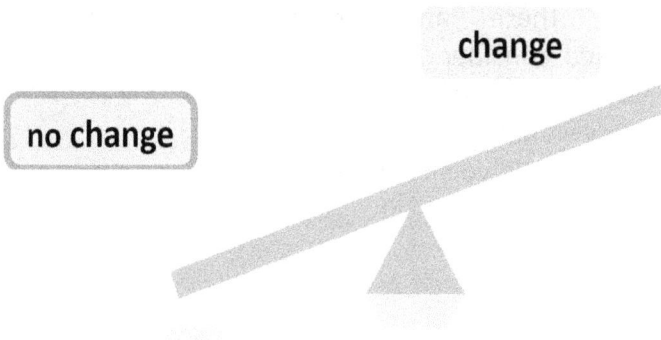

©2010 René Knecht

Present

- How did the need for...arise?
- How does it work now?
- Everything seems fine...or are there any reasons or circumstances in which you would consider an(other) additional partner?
- Is everything going according to plan ... or is there something you would like to change?
- How come you are considering a new supplier? How come you are looking for...?
- (reflectively listening) " Everything is OK...?"

Future

- What are you looking for, instead of ...?
- What would you like to see changed?
- What would you need to know before you switch to a new supplier?
- What do you need to know about us before you can consider us as a new supplier?
- What's important to you about ...?
- How do you know if ...? How would you know that...?
- Which criteria does a supplier need to meet...? What are your criteria for a supplier?
- Are there any circumstances under which you would consider ...?
- What would be the solution for you?
- How would you want to do this?
- How would you like to proceed?

Appendix 2: IT placement (commodity)

Situation

The market for IT placements (secondment) , where IT professionals are hired on a day-to-day basis, is always a commodity market. The demand mainly comes from the client, and the decision-making criteria are more or less fixed. This market is said to be procurement-driven.

Seller:	The seller will first look to find openings. For example: – "How do you currently hire contractors?" – "Is everything running smoothly?"
Client:	"Everything is running smoothly." **Note** Everything is either OK, or the client doesn't want to say.
Seller:	"What profiles are you looking for externally in particular?"
Client:	"IT architects and business analysts."
Seller:	"How many external staff members are there?"
Client:	"30"
Seller:	"When do you use suppliers to hire external staff members?" **Note** Process-oriented question
Client:	"We have large temporary projects, mainly in the banking sector. Former partners referred us to company XYZ. We are currently using three parties."

Seller:	"Can you fill all your positions ...or are there any profiles that you're finding it difficult to fill?" **Note** Technique of the counter-example
Client:	"Yes, it's hard to find IT architects." Note If there wasn't any problem, you wouldn't have been invited.
Seller:	"What steps have you taken to find these staff members?" **Note** Process-oriented question
Client:	"We've approached our other suppliers, but we haven't received anything yet."
Seller:	"What could be the reason for this?"
Client:	"Yeah ... I guess it's quite difficult ... there aren't enough people available."
Seller:	"Suppose you had a supplier that had technical architects available. What would they have to do to be considered?" **Note** Process-oriented question
Client:	"They need to have good CVs, with sound experience in the banking sector. The team is still quite young, so we need someone who's already worked on similar projects."
Seller:	"What will you be looking for when you interview candidates?" **Note** Process-oriented question

Client:	"The suitable candidate also needs some experience of project management, so they can assist the client implement technical solutions. Preferably someone with a software development background." **Note** Answers to process-oriented questions give expert power
Seller:	"If we had someone like this, would you be interested in meeting them?"
Client:	"Yes, but I'd first need to meet with our procurement department. They administer the framework agreements and have to approve any possible collaborations."
Seller:	"OK. Why don't you consult with your procurement department, and if we're approved as a supplier, I can send one of our consultant's CVs and let you know when they're available. Is this a good first step so you can get to know us?" **Note** The contact person might not know how the approval process works, or might not be up to date with internal arrangements. But the seller has introduced a cooperative process that is still under control.
Client:	"Yes..."
Seller:	– "If our candidate's profile is suitable, what would your next step be?"

Continue

The client may ask for examples and references, i.e. returning to the content. So it's important that you maintain a dialogue and ensure there is communication in both directions. We mainly want to demonstrate here how you can achieve this.

It's also important to keep all options open so the client always has freedom of choice. We don't have a monopoly, and the client will show resistance if they don't have freedom to choose.

- ▸ **NOT:** *"Would you prefer A or B?" (The traditional closing)*
- ▷ **BUT:** *"How do you want to proceed? What do you think the next step should be?"*

This enables the seller to keep control over the process, because sending a CV is not entirely without engagement. The *timing* is very important here. Approval by the procurement department is an uncertain factor that often blocks a *deal*. This uncertainty needs be managed while it still can be, so that the negotiation process stays in motion (*process move*). At this stage, because of the timing, the seller has the *process power* to set a counter-requirement, which is used to get the first *commitment*. It's better to require being approved as a potential supplier now, before sending the CV. Otherwise the client can always determine the next step and you lose all power over the sales process.

Remark: the 'time' factor

You can also play with the 'time' factor: if the buyer wants to meet you urgently, you can use this to request a concession, both with regard to context (request prior approval of the price or product feature), and with regard to the process (e.g. meeting another contact person within the organization you want a relationship with). The purpose here is to safeguard the balance in the relationship (*make yourself equal first*), and to not lose any process power.

Remark: give and take

A common strategy for recruiting new clients is to carefully plan and monitor the give and take strategy. You give a little and ask for small commitments in return. This helps to create a relationship and there is a commitment to gradually investigate the relationship further. The seller consciously creates a rhythm for the give and take strategy, and tests the cooperation. Does the client remain cooperative (*compliance mechanism*)?

If you give everything away, when answering a *request for proposals* or if you are invited by the client to introduce yourselves, without asking for anything or a commitment in return, the deal will most probably not go through. (Research amongst our current clients has shown that RFPs without prior contact very rarely lead to a positive outcome. The only reason for responding to an RFP is to advertise your services to possible future contacts.) There is, after all, no dialogue and no cooperation. The rhythm is broken. The change will not take place, because there is insufficient interaction. The client will not change their mind; they will ultimately choose to maintain the status quo (no change) or stick with their (formerly chosen) preferred supplier.

Client:	"We have asked you to come so we can to listen to what you have to offer us." **Note** It can be very tempting to give the client all the reasons why they should collaborate with you, but there is no dialogue. The client will filter all information critically. Unless the client has already decided they want to work with you, this is not a good starting point.
Seller	"Why are you looking for a new supplier? Or "OK ...(pause)... what is the reason that you are now looking for a new supplier? " (This question needs to be asked using a monotonous tone of voice, neutrally and slowly, without exerting any pressure.) **Note** Process-oriented questions that give you back the initiative in a sales discussion. The client also always needs to give their own reasons for wanting to change, not yours! Ego does not sell.

Appendix 3: Selling a financial solution, credit cards

Situation

A seller sells credit cards to companies who spend a lot on travel, and provides solutions for invoicing and managing travel expenses.

Seller:	The seller needs to create a number of openings by asking questions, for example: "How many business travellers are there in your company?" "What are the most important destinations?" "What is your budget for flight tickets?"
Client:	"1 million euro per year" Note This equates to 2000 to 4000 invoices per year, which entails a lot of bookkeeping issues.
Seller:	"How are the flight invoices managed?"
Client:	"The invoices are processed in our accounts and are only paid once they have been approved by the heads of department."
Seller:	"Does the approval process run smoothly?" **Note** The seller asks a question specifically aimed at one of the problem issues.

Client:	"We have someone who works on this fulltime. It's very time-consuming to approve expense sheets, which delays the payments." **Note** It's also possible that the client is not fully aware of the problem. The seller therefore has to ask a series of problem questions to make the client aware. For example: "How long does it take to approve an invoice?" "What's the impact on personnel costs?" "How many invoices aren't paid on time?" "Our clients waste a lot of time on … Is this the same in your organization?" "Are many reminders or legal notices sent?" "How much does this cost?" The seller asks questions that are specifically aimed at the problem issues and their consequences. The confrontation with the facts causes cognitive dissonance. Even though improvements seem to be possible, the client often initially objects to possible change. After all, they have not yet considered it properly. This is one reason why process-oriented questions are so important: see the next question.
Seller:	" What steps have you taken to make this more efficient?" **Note** Process-oriented question

Client:	"We asked our travel agencies to organize the invoicing procedure differently. They are also asking for a solution that would enable them to get paid sooner. They currently always have to pay the airline companies themselves in advance."
Seller:	"Why hasn't this already been resolved?" **Note** Process-oriented question
Client:	**Note** You will receive different and unique answers from every client
Seller:	"How could this be resolved?" Or "What have you done to resolve this?" **Note** Process-oriented question: it is better to leave the client to make a decision. It's a form of *process power,* because it creates commitment.
Client:	"The approval needs to be automated. There are currently too many bottlenecks in the system with invoices being approved by different people. Invoices are often left unprocessed for too long." **Note** The client starts talking about the solution: *change talk*

Seller:	"Would it help to receive all these orders in a single collective account, so that you don't have 200 to 400 separate invoices every month?" **Note** The client will only make a decision about this when it's become clear how this situation was created, and how bad the consequences are (subjective pain or costs). You can only ask suggestive or provocative questions once the client has started talking about *change*. The value of the solution will only become clear once the status quo has been challenged.
Client:	"Yes."
Seller:	"What do you need to implement such a solution?"
Client:	"We would first need to know whether it would be possible to integrate it with our ERP system..."

Appendix 4: Entrepreneurial selling

With *entrepreneurial selling*, we ask the client process-oriented questions from the client's point of view. If you understand the business, you'll be able to sell the concept by creating new opportunities for the client: opportunities that they were not aware of. You basically create a new market for the client. Your process-oriented questioning addresses specific business issues.

The 'give and receive' principle results in **co-creation**. If you focus 100% on the client, the client will grow towards you. The combination of process-oriented sales and focusing on the business is called *entrepreneurial selling*.

Examples

Seller:	"What have you done to approach this sector of the market?"
	"How did the idea to develop this product come about?"
	"What made you decide to reject this productline?"
	"How did you decide to set up this branch?"

These are process-oriented questions that focus on the client's business. This type of question will point the discussion in a specific direction. **The answer is of course unpredictable and unique for every client!**

The only thing you can do is listen and focus on the client, which makes questions like these very powerful. One requirement is that you talk to the *decision-makers* or people who are responsible for results within the organization.

Practice

Take note of the difference between the answers given by the clients for question 1 (product- / content-oriented) and question 2 (process-oriented).

Question 1: content-oriented

Seller:	"How are you currently attracting new clients?"
Client:	"We have 4 account managers who are responsible for a region."

Question 2: process-oriented

Seller:	"How do clients choose you as their supplier?"
Client:	"Our clients are automation companies who rely on us because they use our standard components to quickly implement their solutions in manufacturing companies. They can deliver faster thanks to our technology."

Process-oriented questions provide a different type of information, which make consulting with your client much more agreeable. You enter into a dialogue and interesting possibilities come to the fore quite quickly. You will certainly have a better understanding of the client. It's interesting that answers to process-oriented questions are often **unpredictable,** so you are forced to listen. This enables you to evolve from product differentiation to business differentiation (client's client).

Product differentiation

The central question here is: **"How can the client's situation improve?"** Answers include, for example: reducing costs, increasing efficiency or more profits. The seller is the expert or *facilitator.* The following questions are more contextual, so not process-oriented. It is these types of questions that must be used for solution-oriented sales.

Seller:	"On average, how long does it take for clients to pay their invoices?"
	"Who follows up late payments?" "How much would it be worth if your invoices were paid an average of 30 days earlier?" "What are you doing to ensure your clients pay on time?"

Business differentiation

The central question here is: **"How can my client create value for their clients?"**

This perspective focuses more on the business needs of the client's client. The seller becomes a co-entrepreneur. These apparently easy questions do not differentiate as such; it is the **answers that co-create.**

The following questions are business- and so process-oriented:

Seller:	*Business-orientated questions:* "How important is credit for your clients?" "Your clients are enterprises with a high number of transactions and low profit margins. How would you be able to help them cut down their credit expenses?"
	"You build websites. How do your clients try to reach their target groups via websites? How do you help your clients to increase their turnover? How do you help your clients reach their clients?"
	Process-oriented questions: "How do clients choose you as their supplier?"
	"What make clients decide to do business with you?" "Why do clients want to do business with you?" "You are awarded major government projects. Why are you so successful with the government?" "How do you define your ideal client profile?" "Who were your first clients?" "How were those contacts established?"

We can formulate process-oriented questions from the 'client's client' perspective. These process-oriented questions focus 100% on the client and on their decision-making process.

Appendix 5: Selling value: the 'Differentiation'

'Value' is the extent to which you are better at meeting your client's needs / expectations than their alternative. The alternative can be one of your direct competitors or the status quo (does nothing or does it on their own).

It follows from this that value:

> ▷ is created in the selling process. This process is a 2-way interaction. The seller leads this process so the client is forced to consider their past decision and current options.
> ▷ is created by comparing and questioning the alternatives, including the status quo.

Because the creation of value is a step-by-step process, and we want to reach a decision, sellers are always required to 'guide' this process. The client rarely does this of their own accord (unless they have already decided to 'change', which is hardly ever the case with cold acquisition).

Tips for selling the value of change

1. **Start by challenging decisions that were made in the past**
   Do not start by reverting to old sales methods and talking about your presentation or about the content of your solution (which is very tempting, but won't attract the client!) The market is suffering from solutions fatigue. Allow the client to consider first. They need to start by getting their own thoughts in order.

   "How did this project start?",

   "How did you start working together?",

   "Why we are sitting together and have a meeting today?"

2. **Know and accept that the client decides**
   Value is something that the client makes a decision about, so they have to understand this for themselves. This is the most effective way of approaching the client. We assume the

intrinsic motivation of the client; they can and want to make their own decision. Decision-makers are mainly intrinsically motivated. They rely on themselves, and that's what they're paid to do.

3. **Run through the alternatives**
   Before giving any of your 'solution' away, let the client question their past decisions and current options.

   "Can your current supplier not help you with this?",
   "Why are you still looking?",
   "What is the reason that you are still looking for...?"

The magical result is that the client will ask about what expertise you can offer to solve their problem. So don't worry: your offer or solution will be discussed. It is this impatience or anxiety about losing control that causes sellers to exert pressure on clients and put them off (which also emphasizes the value of the status quo to the client: "we aren't ready for this").

'How?' comes before 'What?'

**– you guide the meeting;
the client makes decisions and commitments**

IX: Bibliography and references

BIBLIOGRAPHY AND SOURCES OF INSPIRATION

I found most of my inspiration from my personal experiences as a seller, recruiter and trainer. I tested my insights against a number of interesting theories developed by experts in the domains summarized below. As experts in their domain, their unique vision can help develop knowledge and understanding. You will also find a number of references at the bottom that have a more academic background, for readers who want their experience to have a more scientific basis.

Bibliography

Conflict management

* DANA, D., Conflict Resolution, Mediation Tools for Everyday Work life, McGraw-Hill, New York, 2000.
* CRAWLEY, J., GRAHAM, K., Mediation for Managers, Nicolas Brealy Publishing, London, 2002.
* BELKSMA, T., Mediation in de praktijk; wat houdt mediation in, aan de hand van een achttal cases, Mediation, Alphen aan de Rijn, 1999.
* APOL, G.R.A., BELKSMA, W.A., REIJERKERK, L.J., VAN DER HOEK, J.C., Mediation Trainingsinstituut MTI, Praktijkgids Mediation 2006, Kluwer Onderwijs, Deventer, 2006.
* MACHIAVELLI, N, De Heerser, Athenaeum-Polak & Van Gennep, Amsterdam, 1988.
* ACHTERHUIS, RABBIE, VROON, WIEPKEMA, WILTERDINK, PROCEE (red.), Het beest in de mens, Uitgeverij Ambo, Baarn, 1994.
* FRITCHIE, R.,MALCOLM, L., Conflictoplossing op het werk, Uitgeverij Nieuwezijds, 2000 (translation).
* GLASL, F., Help! Conflicten, Heb ik een conflict of heeft het conflict mij, Vrij Geestesleven, Zeist, 2001.

* DE VOS, L., Strategie en Tactiek. Inleiding tot de moderne krijgsgeschiedenis, Davidsfonds, Leuven, 2006.

Sales

* KNECHT, R., Differentiation Selling, de methode om via het verkoopsproces het verschil te maken, Kluwer, Mechelen, Belgium, 2011.
* KNECHT, R, Differentiation Selling, ICT-Connecting bvba, Gent, Belgium, 2010.
* RACKHAM, N., SPIN Selling, McGraw-Hill, New York, 1988.
* RACKHAM? N., DEVINCENTIS J., Rethinking the Sales Force, Redefining Selling to Create and Capture Customer Value, McGraw-Hill, New York, 1999.
* EADES, K.M., The New Solution Selling, Solution Selling Inc, McGraw-Hill, USA, 2004.
* BOSWORTH, M., HOLLAND, J., Customer Centric Selling, McGraw-Hill, USA, 2004.
* SNYDERT, K., KEARNS, K., Escaping the Price-Driven Sale, Huthwaite Inc, McGraw-Hill Companies, New York, 2008.
* HEIMAN, S., SANCHEZ, D., TULEJA, T., Strategic Selling, Miller Heiman Inc, Reno, 1995-1998.
* MORGEN, S., D., Buying Facilitation: the New Way to Sell That Influences and Expands Decisions, Morgan Publishing, Naples, 1994.
* TRACY, B., *The Psychology of Selling*, Nelson Business, Nashville, 2004.
* DEEP, S., SUSSMAN, L., Sandler Sales Institute, *Close the Deal*, Perseus Publishing, Massachusetts, 1999.
* DAVID, S., *You Can't Teach a Kid to Ride a Bike at a Seminar*, Bay Head Publishing Inc, 4e druk, Owing Mills, 2003.
* MATTSON, D., PARINELLO, A., *Five Minutes With VITO*, Sandler Systems Inc, Anthony Parinello, 2009.

* THOMSON, A. H., ROSLER, *The Feldman Method*, Longman Group USA INC, Chicago Illinois, 1989 (The disturbing questions technique stemmed from the legendary insurance salesman, Feldman, in the '50s.)

* BURNS, B., SNYDER, T., *Selling in a New Market Space*, McGraw-Hill, USA, 2010 (Contains interesting views on managing the sales process using a negotiation approach.)

* VERBEKE, W., *Het verkopen van kennis*, Pearson Education Benelux, Amsterdam, 2005.

* VERBEKE, W., *Het succesvol shapen van key accounts*, Pearson Education Benelux, Rotterdam, 2008.

* DAVIS, K., *Slow Down, Sell Faster*, American Management Association, United States, 2011.

* DIXON, M., ADAMSON, B., *The Challenger Sale, Taking Control of the Customer Conversation*, Penguin, United States, 2011.

* BUZAN, T., ISRAEL, R., *Sales genius*, Gower Publishing Limited, Surrey, 2000.

* READ, N., BISTRITZS, S., *Selling to the C-Suite*, McGraw-Hill, New York, 2010.

* SEARCY, T., *RFPs Suck!, How to Master the RFP System Once and for All to Win Big Business*, Channel V Books, United States, 2009.

* HOLDEN J., KUBACKI, R., *The New Power Base Selling, Master the Politics, Create Unexpected Value and Higher Margins, and Outsmart the Competition*, John Wiley & Sons, Hoboken – New Jersey, Inc., 2012.

* LUEFSCHUETZ, G., *Selling Professional Services to the Fortune 500: how to win in the billion-dollar market of strategy consulting, technology solutions, and outsourcing services*, McGraw-Hill, New York, 2010.

* SALACUSE, J.W., *The Art of Advice, How to Give It and How to Take It*, Times Books, New York, 1994. The author also discusses using the three time dimensions (past, present, future) to understand your client (p. 36, p. 58).

Cold calling

- GALPER, A., *Unlock-The-Game*, Mastery Program, 2004. A multi-media program that I bought in 2004, which teaches you how to make cold calls and create a dialogue with prospective clients.
- KONRATH, J., *Selling to Big Companies*, Dearborn Trade Publishing, Chicago, 2006. The emphasis is on selling the pain to make appointments.
- KONRATH, J., *SNAP Selling*, Penguin Group, USA, 2010. This book describes how *consultative selling* is 'dead', partly due to commoditization and the client's lack of time. There is after all no time and space for dialogue.

Leadership

- COVEY, S.R., *De zeven eigenschappen van effectief leiderschap*, Uitgeverij Business Contact, Amsterdam, 2002.
- COVEY, S.R., *De 8ste eigenschap*, Uitgeverij Business Contact, Amsterdam, 2008. Management guru Covey gives very good examples of what active listening entails.
- MASLOW, A., *Motivation and Personality*, second edition, Harper & Row, Publishers, Inc., New York, 1970.
- BAAN, J., *De weg naar marktleiderschap, Mijn leven als ondernemer*, Pearson Education, Benelux, 2005
- GODIN, Seth, *De Dip*, AW Bruna LeV, 2007. Godin explains that breakthroughs need to be enforced. Our reptile brains will always show resistance to innovations or change. Our society is be permeated with this attitude and so always strive for mediocrity. The correlation with selling lies in the fact that we, as sellers, are also confronted with these resistances when we approach organizations with our solutions.

Body language

* PEASE, A., Body Language. How to read others' thoughts by their gestures, Sheldon Press, London, 1984.
* Business and economy
* TRACY, B., *The 100 Absolutely Unbreakable Laws of Business Success*, Berrett-Koehler Publishers INC, San Francisco, 2000.
* Brian Tracy has the ability to explain complex matters in detail. I found his interpretation of the laws of economy (which he describes as the laws of psychology of '*humans in action*') refreshing, even to me as an economist. I had never looked at things from this perspective before.
* TRACY, B., *Something for nothing, The Causes and Cures of All our Problems and What You can Do to Save the American Dream* , Executive Books, Mechanicsburg, US, 2004. An excellent approach to the economic behavior of humans, described as selfish, vain, impatient ... This *expediency factor* is approached positively, because it forms the basis of progress, but it is also a statement of what is lacking in our society.
* D'AVENI, R., *Omgaan met Hyperconcurrentie met behulp van het nieuwe 7S-raamwerk*, Management Briefing, Academic Service, Schoonhoven, 1995 *(translation of the article 'Coping with Hypercompetition: Utilizing the new 7S's framework' published in Academy of Management Executive, 1995, Vol.9 No.3 pp. 45-57)*.
* ELFRING, T., *Innovatief ondernemerschap*, Management Briefing, Schoonhoven, 2000.

Systems Thinking, Change Management, Behavioral Changes, Education

- ROGERS, C., *Client Centered therapy*, Houghton-Mifflin, Boston, 1961.
- DILTS, R., *Hierarchy of Criteria*, www.nlpu.com/ archive.htm, Santa Cruz CA, 1998. Dilts is one of the pioneers of NLP. In this article, he describes a number of examples of *Criteria Elicitation* that can be used as inspiration.
- SCHEIN, E., *Organisational Culture and Leadership*, Jossey-Bass, San Francisco, 2010.
- SCHEIN, E., *Process Consulting Revisited, Building the Helping Relationship*, Addison-Wesley Publishing Company, United States, 1999.
- MILLER, W., ROLLNICK, S., *Motivational Interviewing*, The Guilford Press, New York, 2002.
- ROSENGREN, D., *Building Motivational Interviewing Skills, a practitioner workbook*, The Guilford Press, New York, 2009.
- VAN DER GEER, P., Peters, R., *In plaats van praten, Debat en dialoog bij veranderprocessen*, Het Spectrum, Utrecht, 2004
- KOLB, D., *Experiential Learning Experience as The Source of Learning and Development*, Prentice Hall Inc, New Jersey, 1984.
- Putz, G., *Facilitation Skills, Helping Groups Make Decisions*, second edition Deep Space Technology Company, US, 2002.
- KNIGHT, S., *NLP Solutions, How to model what works in business to make it work for you*, Nicholas Brealey Publishing, London, 1999.
- KNIGHT, S., *NLP at Work, The Difference that Makes a Difference in Business*, second edition, Nicholas Brealey Publishing, London, 2002.
- BULLMER, K., *The Art of Empathy, A Manual for Improving Accuracy of Interpersonal Perception*, Human Sciences Press, New York, 1975.

* BEKMAN, A., *Adviseren, Het geheim van de smid*, 3de druk, Koninklijke Van Gorcum BV, Assen, 2002. Adriaan Bekman is an business advisor who helped me understand that change always happens in a moment of standstill. It is an input process, not an output process. It cannot be imposed or arranged. I have always remembered these words and they still influence my thoughts today.

* OSHO, *Intuition , Knowing Beyond Logic*, Osho International Foundation, 2001.

* KETS DE VRIES, M, BALAZS, K., *De menselijke kant van reorganiseren*, Academic Service, Schoonhoven, 1996 (NL translation 1996 Holland Management Review, European Management Journal, Vol. 14 M.F.R., Thu Human Side of Downsizing pp. 111-120).

* CULLEN , D, *Afscheid van Maslow's Motivatietheorie*, Management Briefing, Academic Service Schoonhoven (NL translation of 'Maslow, Monkeys and Motivation Theory' in Organisation, volume 4 (3), Sage , London, Thousand Oaks, and New Delhi 1997).

* Schein, E., *Drie Managementculturen, De sleutel tot bedrijfsleerprocessen*, Academic Service, Schoonhoven (translation 'Three Cultures of Management: The Key to Organizational Learning' by Edgard H. Schein, Sloan Management Review, Fall 1996, pp. 9-20.

* BUZAN, T., B., The Mindmap Book, BBC Books, London, 1995.

* DE BONO, E., Eenvoud, 'Simplicity', translated by M. Hoogeboom, Uitgeverij Nieuwezijds, 1999.

Negotiation

* KORDA, P., (2010), *Négocier et défendre ses marges*, Dundod, Paris, 2010.

* RUIJTER, F., *Persoonlijk onderhandelen*, Pearson Education Benelux, 2004.

* GUTH, S., *The Contract Negotiation Handbook, An Indispensable Guide for Contract Professionals*, Lulu Press, Inc., US 2008.

- BRAGG, M., *Invloed en Macht*, 'Reinventing Influence', translated by Peter van der Kaaij, Uitgeverij Contact, Amsterdam, 1996.

- KENNEDY, G., *Strategic Negotiation*, Gower Publishing Limited, Hampshire, England, 2007.

- KENNEDY, G., *The New Negotiation Edge, The Behavioural Approach for Results and Relationships*, Nicholas Brealey Publishing, London, 1998.

- ENS International, *Professional Negotiating and Influencing: an ENS International reference Manual*, ENS International, 6th edition, Sydney, 2002.

- GOOVAERTS, L., *Onderhandelen voor alledag*, Auxis, Brussels, 1999.

- FISCHER, R., URY, W., PATTON, B., *Excellent onderhandelen* ⬜ *The Harvard Negotiation Project*, 'Getting to Yes', translated by Hugo Kuipers and Paul Duchateau, Uitgeverij Business Contact, Amsterdam, 2002. translation

- CIALDINI, R., *Influence,* Harper Collins College Publishers, New York, 1993.

- KARASS, C., *The Negotiation Game, How to Get What You Want, Revised Edition,* Harper Business – HarperCollins Publishers Inc., United States, 1992.

- DIETMEYER, B., *B2B Street Fighting, Next Generation Business-to-Business Negotiation*, Think! Inc., United States, 2011.

- MASTENBROEK, W., *Negotiation as Emotion Management*, Holland Business Publications, Heemstede, 2002.

Psychology

- BREHM, S., KASSIN, S., FEIN, S., *Social Psychology*, Houghton Mifflin Company, Boston, 1999.

- KNOWLES, E. S., LINN, J.A., *Resistance and Persuasion*, Lawrence Erlbaum Associates Inc, New Jersey, 2004.

- BERNE, dr. E., *Mens Erger JE Niet, De psychologie van de intermenselijke verhoudingen*, Uitgeverij Bert Bakker, Amsterdam, 1967.

- LINDSTROM, M., *buy.ology, Truth and Lies About Why We Buy*, Broadway Books (the Crown Publishing Group), New York, 2008.

- RENVOISE P., MORIN, C., *Neuromarketing, Understanding the 'Buy Button' in Your Customer's Brain*, Thomas Nelson, Nashville-Tennessee, 2007.

- PRADEEP, Dr. A.K., *The Buying Brain, Secrets for Selling to the Subconscious Mind*, John Wiley & Sons, Inc., Hoboken-New Jersey, 2010 .

- BUZAN, T., *De kracht van Sociale Intelligentie*, Thema, business science and educational publisher, Zaltbommel, 2003.

- GARDNER, H., Frames of Mind, The Theory of Multiple Intelligences, Basic Books (A Member of the Perseus Books Group), United States, 1983,2004,2011.

- GOLEMAN, D., *Emotionele intelligentie in de praktijk*, Uitgeverij Contact, Amsterdam, 1998.

Cognitive dissonance and decision-making

* FESTINGER, L., *Conflict, Decision, and Dissonance*, Stanford University Press, Stanford, California, 1964. Festinger's traditional studies, which are often referred to in discussions, look into cognitive dissonance in the *post-decision* phase (the so-called doubt after buying). This is also applicable to Festinger, who assumes that the decision-making process takes place rather rationally in the pre-decision phase, where alternatives and considered and weighed up according to a rational process before a final decision is taken. I cannot generalize his studies with students in a sales context.

* MILAN, Z., *Multiple Criteria Decision Making*, McGraw-Hill Book Company, hoofdstuk3, New York, 1981. Here, decision-making is viewed as a process with sub-decisions that create CD. There is conflict because there is no such thing as an ideal solution. The client therefore needs to reject and look for new alternatives, and adjust their criteria. The sub-decisions always cause CD. After all, an alternative is always eliminated. There is interaction between CD and conflict. I also think this is the point of view that correlates most closely with my B-to-B sales experience: every *post-decision* phase forms a pre-decision phase in the continuum of all sub-decisions. Selling is, after all, a continuous process: as soon as (sub-)decision has been taken, you are preparing for the next decision.

* JANIS, I., MANN, L., *Decision Making, A Psychological Analysis of Conflict, Choice, and* Commitment, The Free Press, A Division of Macmillan Publishing Co. Inc, New York, 1977.

Communication

* NELISSEN, P.L.C., JONKERS, J.W.J., MANDERS, Th.G.W.M., Massacommunicatie, een TIJDopname ten behoeve van de reclame, Instituut voor Toegepaste Sociologie, Nijmegen, 1970. Chapter 3 contains interesting conclusions about changes in attitude that are also relevant to personal sales.

* BURTON, J., BODENHAMER DMin, B. G. ,Hypnotic Language, Its Structure and Use, Crown House Publishing , UK , 2000. A number of interesting contributions about how someone becomes susceptible to new ideas by creating cognitive dissonance, and how this can be used in language patterns. Questions can be used to direct the focus inwards. In this mildy trance-like state (narrowing of consciousness), you are more susceptible to suggestions from the outside. The recipient is less critical, which is also the essence of effective negotiating: creating a cooperative climate so that it is easier to influence the other party.

* KNECHT, J., STOELINGA, B. G. J., Communicatiebegrippenlijst, Kluwer Bedrijfswetenschappen, Deventer, Tweede geheel herziene druk, 1992.

X: About Author

Brief description

Differentiation Selling® teaches sellers to differentiate themselves in the selling process using easy procedures and questioning techniques. Practical examples are used to demonstrate how you can employ process-oriented questions in a sales discussion.

Extracts from this book

"Clients today are not looking for a solution, but a supplier. This means selling is about breaking the status quo, either by changing the working method or changing the current supplier."

"As a seller, you start by creating conflict in the organization you want to sell to: to change or not to change?"

"Process-oriented questions help the client to break existing buying patterns and that's what hunting (cold acquisition) is all about!"

"The secret to effective influencing has always been about allowing clients to make their own decisions."

About the author

René Knecht gained a master's degree in Commercial Engineering from the Vrije Universiteit Brussel (University of Brussels, Belgium) and quickly excelled in sales. In 1999, he switched to HR consultancy in recruitment and training, which, in 2005, led to the incorporation of his company, ICT-Connecting: a specialist direct search agency for ICT and sales roles.

René developed the Differentiation Selling concept in 2009. The concept is based on *best practices* in sales, negotiation, change management, conflict management, and interviews with over 1500 sales and account managers since 1999.

René Knecht

Mail: rene.knecht@differentiationselling.com

             info@differentiationselling.com

Web: www.differentiationselling.com

LinkedIn: http://be.linkedin.com/in/reneknecht

Twitter: http://twitter.com/ReneKnecht

ICT-Connecting bvba

Phone +32 497 48 38 52 - Fax + 32 9 330 40 33

Jozef Plateaustraat 11 9000 Ghent – Belgium

VAT BE 0881 964 976

www.ingramcontent.com/pod-product-compliance
Lightning Source LLC
Chambersburg PA
CBHW071117210326
41519CB00020B/6327